Nicole Routhier

Vietnamese

D1157370

NICOLE ROUTHIER

Vietnamese

Photography by Simon Wheeler

WEIDENFELD & NICOLSON

Nicole Routhier

Nicole Routhier was born in Vietnam, and trained at the Culinary Institute of America. She is one of the most popular cookery writers in the United States, and is considered the foremost authority on Vietnamese cuisine.

She has written several books, including *Cooking Under Wraps*, *Nicole Routhier's Fruit Cookbook* and *The Foods of Vietnam*, which won both The James Beard Foundation and the Institute of American Culinary Professionals Cookbook of the Year awards in 1991.

Nicole Routhier lives in Houston, Texas, where she owns a restaurant consulting practice and teaches Southeast Asian cooking.

Photograph by Anthony Laudin

Contents

In all aspects of life, in no place should indifference be allowed to creep; and nowhere less than the domain of the culinary arts.

YUAN WEI
(18th-century Chinese gourmet and philosopher)

Introduction

For decades, Vietnamese cooking was one of Asia's best-kept culinary secrets. Only recently has the rest of the world come to appreciate its exquisite delicacy of flavours, achieved through the artful blending of herbs and spices.

This book highlights some of the most representative dishes of Vietnamese cuisine. Although Vietnamese food is firmly rooted in a 2,000-year-old culinary tradition, I have made an effort to adapt the recipes for the contemporary kitchen. I have chosen dishes that are appealing and yet easy to prepare, and that offer variety so that you can build complete meals from the recipes in this book. In so doing, you will begin to capture the true spirit of the Vietnamese diet, which is naturally light and healthy.

I hope these recipes will serve as an introduction to the exciting (but often misunderstood) world of Vietnamese food, and an inspiration to further explore its virtues.

Bon appétit!

GA LUI
Skewered five-spice chicken

MAKES 48 SKEWERS

8 boned and skinned chicken
  breasts (about 900 g/2 lb),
  trimmed and halved

Marinade

1 shallot, chopped

3 large garlic cloves, chopped

1 thick stalk of lemongrass,
  peeled and thinly sliced

2 tablespoons sugar

½ teaspoon chilli paste

1 tablespoon fish sauce

1 tablespoon soy sauce

1 tablespoon sesame seed oil

2 tablespoons peanut or
  vegetable oil

1 teaspoon five-spice powder

To serve

Chilli dipping sauce (page 36)

Place all the ingredients for the marinade in a liquidizer
or food processor and blend until finely puréed. Transfer
to a large mixing bowl.

Cut each of the chicken breasts lengthwise into four
strips. Lightly pound the strips to 1 cm/½ inch thick,
using a meat mallet or the flat side of a cleaver. Cut
the strips in half and add them to the marinade. Toss
well to coat all the strips thoroughly, then cover and
leave to marinate at room temperature for 1 hour, or
overnight in the refrigerator.

Soak 48 bamboo skewers in salted hot water for
30 minutes.

Prepare the barbecue or preheat the grill. Thread a slice
of chicken on to each skewer.

Grill the skewers, turning once, until the chicken is
browned on both sides and cooked through, about
3–4 minutes. Serve immediately, passing the Chilli
dipping sauce separately.

*Serve as an appetizer, or as a main course as part of a family
meal. Accompany with steamed rice, a sautéed vegetable such
as green beans, and a bowl of soup.*

CHA GIO
Fried spring rolls

MAKES 25–30 ROLLS

200 g/7 oz sugar
25–30 dried rice papers (page 35)
peanut oil for frying

Filling

6 dried shiitake mushrooms,
    soaked in boiling water for
    30 minutes, finely chopped
25 g/1 oz cellophane (bean
    thread) noodles, soaked in
    hot water for 30 minutes, cut
    into 2.5 cm/1 inch lengths
1 large chicken breast (about
    275 g/10 oz), chopped
275 g/10 oz uncooked prawns,
    shelled and coarsely chopped
125 g/4 oz minced pork
85 g/3 oz beansprouts, chopped
2–3 carrots, grated
1 onion, finely chopped
2–3 garlic cloves, finely chopped
4 tablespoons fish sauce
2 teaspoons sugar
½ teaspoon salt
pepper
3 eggs

To serve

plenty of soft-leaved lettuce,
    fresh coriander and mint
double quantity of Chilli dipping
    sauce (page 36)

To make the filling, put the chopped mushrooms and noodles in a large bowl. Add all the remaining ingredients and mix thoroughly with your hands.

To assemble the rolls, fill a large bowl with 2 litres/3½ pints hot water and dissolve the sugar in it. Work with one sheet of rice paper at a time, keeping the remaining sheets covered with a barely damp cloth. Immerse the rice paper in the hot water, then quickly remove and lay it flat on a damp tea towel.

Fold up the bottom third of the rice paper. Place 4 tablespoons of filling in the centre of the folded–over portion. Shape the filling into a log about 15 cm/6 inches long. Fold in the right and left sides of the rice paper over the mixture. Roll up the rice paper from bottom to top to enclose the filling. Place the filled rolls, seam side down, in a single layer on a baking sheet. (These can be prepared ahead, covered and refrigerated.)

Preheat the oven to 120°C/250°F/Gas Mark ½. If possible, use two large frying pans to fry the rolls. Pour about 5 cm/2 inches of oil into each pan and heat to 165°C/330°F (well below smoking point). Add some rolls to each pan (do not crowd or they will stick together) and fry for 10–12 minutes, turning often, until crisp and browned. Drain on paper towels. Keep warm in the oven while you fry the remaining rolls.

To serve, cut each roll in half with a serrated knife. Wrap in a lettuce leaf, along with some coriander and mint, and dip into the Chilli dipping sauce.

Serve as an appetizer, or as buffet food for a special occasion.

NOM GIA
Beansprouts and crabmeat salad

**SERVES 6 AS A STARTER OR ABOUT
40 AS A BUFFET DISH**

1 large garlic clove, finely
    chopped
2 fresh red chillies, finely
    chopped
1 tablespoon sugar
1 tablespoon fresh lime juice
1 tablespoon rice vinegar or
    distilled white vinegar
3 tablespoons fish sauce
2 tablespoons peanut or
    vegetable oil
1 carrot, shredded
1 small cucumber, peeled,
    halved lengthwise, seeded
    and thinly sliced
1 teaspoon salt
450 g/1 lb fresh beansprouts
325 g/12 oz fresh or canned
    crabmeat, well picked over
4 tablespoons coarsely chopped
    fresh coriander leaves
2 tablespoons coarsely ground
    roasted peanuts (page 36)
2 tablespoons coarsely ground
    toasted sesame seeds
    (page 36)

Whisk together the garlic, chillies, sugar, lime juice, vinegar, fish sauce and oil in a small mixing bowl. Set aside.

Toss the carrot and cucumber in a colander with the salt, and leave to stand for 15 minutes. Rinse under cold running water and squeeze dry with your hands (it is very important that the vegetables are completely dry to ensure that they remain crunchy).

Place the carrot and cucumber in a large bowl and add the remaining ingredients. Pour the dressing over the salad and toss until well combined.

This salad is excellent for parties. Serve with prawn crackers (page 34), so that bite-sized portions of the salad can be picked up on the crackers and eaten with the hands. Follow with sticky rice and chicken (page 22) or beef curry (page 28).

BUN TOM
Rice noodles with stir-fried prawns

SERVES 4

450 g/1 lb uncooked prawns,
shelled, deveined and halved
lengthwise
2 teaspoons fish sauce
1 large garlic clove, finely
chopped
pepper
225 g/8 oz dried rice sticks
(*banh pho*, 5 mm/¼ inch
wide), soaked in warm water
for 30 minutes, drained
200 g/7 oz fresh beansprouts,
rinsed and drained
1 tablespoon peanut or
vegetable oil
2 shallots, thinly sliced
½ red pepper, seeded and cut
into thin strips
4 spring onions, thinly sliced
50 g/2 oz roasted peanuts,
coarsely ground (page 36)
double quantity of Chilli dipping
sauce (page 36)

To garnish
sprigs of coriander

In a bowl, combine the prawns with the fish sauce, garlic and some freshly ground black pepper. Cover and leave to marinate in the refrigerator for 30 minutes.

Bring 2 litres/3½ pints water to the boil in a large saucepan, add a good pinch of salt, then drop in the drained noodles. After the water returns to the boil, cook until the noodles are just tender: no more than 1 minute. Immediately remove the pan from the heat and stir in the beansprouts. Drain into a colander and refresh under cold running water. Drain well.

Heat the oil in a wok or large frying pan over high heat. Add the shallots and stir-fry until soft. Add the prawns and their marinade and stir-fry until they turn pink and curl, about 1 minute. Add the red pepper and spring onions and cook for a further 1 minute, then remove from the heat.

Put the noodle mixture in a large bowl, add the stir-fried prawns and ground peanuts, drizzle the Chilli dipping sauce over and toss thoroughly. Serve immediately, garnished with coriander.

This is a complete meal-in-one-dish, but if you like you could precede it with a light vegetable soup.

CANH CHUA CA
Hot and sour fish soup

SERVES 4

4 sea bass fillets, about 125 g/
    4 oz each
4 tablespoons fish sauce
pepper
1 tablespoon vegetable oil
1 small onion, halved and sliced
2 large garlic cloves, finely
    chopped
2 fresh red chillies, finely
    chopped, or ½ teaspoon chilli
    paste
4 plum tomatoes, quartered
    lengthwise and seeded
½ small pineapple, cubed
2 tablespoons sugar
1 teaspoon salt
a large handful of fresh
    beansprouts
1 stick of celery, thinly sliced
2 tablespoons fresh lime juice
1 heaped tablespoon chopped
    fresh mint

Place the fish in a shallow dish, then sprinkle with 1 tablespoon fish sauce and some freshly ground black pepper. Cover and leave in the refrigerator.

Heat the oil in a large saucepan. Add the onion, garlic and chillies and stir-fry until fragrant, about 30 seconds. Add the tomatoes, pineapple and sugar, and cook until the tomatoes begin to soften, about 1 minute.

Stir in 1.2 litres/2 pints hot water, the salt and the remaining 3 tablespoons fish sauce, then bring to the boil. Reduce the heat to moderate and simmer the broth, covered, for 5 minutes.

Add the fish, beansprouts and celery, then immediately remove the pan from the heat. Cover and leave to stand for 5 minutes, to finish cooking the fish and allow the flavours to marry. Stir in the lime juice and mint just before serving.

Round off the meal with steamed rice and charcoal-grilled pork chops (page 30).

Tom xao gung
Stir-fried prawns with honey and ginger

SERVES 4

2 tablespoons peanut oil

450 g/1 lb uncooked large
  prawns, shelled and deveined

1 large onion, halved and thinly
  sliced

6 large garlic cloves, thinly sliced

1 heaped tablespoon thinly
  shredded fresh ginger

½ red pepper, seeded and cut
  lengthwise into thin strips

2 tablespoons honey

1 tablespoon fish sauce

1 tablespoon soy sauce

½ teaspoon five-spice powder

pepper

To garnish

sprigs of coriander

Heat 1 tablespoon of the oil in a large frying pan over high heat. Add the prawns and stir-fry until they turn pink but are not cooked through, about 1 minute. Using a slotted spoon, transfer the prawns to a bowl.

Add the remaining oil to the same pan and heat. Add the onion, garlic and ginger and stir-fry until browned and soft, about 3 minutes. Add the pepper and cook for a further 1 minute. Stir in the honey, fish sauce, soy sauce, five-spice powder and prawns. Toss to combine all the ingredients and cook until the prawns are evenly glazed with the sauce, about 2 minutes. Transfer to a warm platter, sprinkle with freshly ground black pepper and garnish with coriander. Serve at once.

Accompany with a simple sautéed vegetable, such as green beans or sugar snap peas, and rice. Pickled vegetables (page 37) would also make a fine accompaniment to this dish.

XOI GA
Sticky rice and chicken

SERVES 4–6

275 g/10 oz glutinous (sticky) rice, soaked in water to cover for 4 hours, or overnight

225 g/8 oz mung dhal (dried mung bean halves without skins), soaked in water to cover for 4 hours, or overnight

½ teaspoon salt

2 chicken breasts (about 325 g/ 12 oz), skinned and cubed

1 large garlic clove, finely chopped

1 tablespoon fish sauce

½ teaspoon sugar

1 tablespoon vegetable oil

6 spring onions, thinly sliced

pepper

Drain the rice and beans and wash until the water runs clear. Mix the rice and beans with the salt and spread the mixture over a dampened piece of muslin in the top of a steamer. Steam above gently boiling water for 30–40 minutes, sprinkling water over the mixture frequently, until the rice is tender and the beans can be easily crushed with your fingertips.

While the rice is cooking, combine the chicken, garlic, fish sauce and sugar in a small bowl, and leave to marinate for 10 minutes.

Heat the oil in a large frying pan over high heat. Add the chicken and stir-fry until browned and tender, about 3 minutes. Add the spring onions and stir for a further 30 seconds. Mix the chicken into the rice-and-bean mixture. Sprinkle with freshly ground black pepper and serve immediately.

Beansprouts and crabmeat salad (page 14) would be a perfect accompaniment to this hearty dish (the crabmeat may be omitted if you like). Pass Chilli dipping sauce (page 36) to sprinkle over the rice.

CA CHIEN SOT CA CHUA
Pan-fried sea bass with spicy tomato sauce

SERVES 4

3 tablespoons peanut or
    vegetable oil
4 shallots, thinly sliced
4 large garlic cloves, thinly sliced
4 large ripe tomatoes (about
    675 g/1½ lb), cored, seeded
    and coarsely chopped
2 fresh red chillies, finely
    chopped, or ½ teaspoon chilli
    paste
2 tablespoons fish sauce, plus 2
    teaspoons
1 teaspoon sugar
2 spring onions, thinly sliced
2 tablespoons chopped fresh dill
125 g/4 oz plain flour
4 sea bass or red snapper fillets,
    about 175 g/6 oz each
pepper

Heat 2 tablespoons of the oil in a large frying pan over moderate heat. Add the shallots and garlic and stir-fry until fragrant, about 30 seconds. Add the tomatoes and chillies and stir-fry for 1 minute. Add 2 tablespoons of the fish sauce, the sugar, and 4 tablespoons water. Cover and simmer for 5 minutes, stirring occasionally.

Stir in the spring onions and dill, then remove the pan from the heat. Cover to keep the sauce warm while you cook the fish.

Sift the flour on to a large platter. Pat the fish dry and make a few diagonal slits on the skin side at the thickest part of each fillet. Rub the fillets with the remaining 2 teaspoons fish sauce and sprinkle with black pepper, then dredge in the flour, shaking off any excess. Place the fish on a platter.

Heat a large nonstick frying pan over high heat for 15 seconds, then add the remaining 1 tablespoon oil. When the oil is smoking hot, carefully add the fish, skin side down. Reduce the heat to medium–high, cover the pan and cook until the skin is crisp and golden brown, about 5 minutes. Using two wide metal spatulas, carefully turn the fish. Continue to cook, uncovered, for 1 minute, or until the fish flakes easily when tested with a fork. Transfer the fish to a large platter. Ladle the tomato sauce over the fish and serve immediately.

For a complete main course, all that is needed is a bowl of rice, a soup, and a steamed vegetable, such as asparagus or spinach. Pass Chilli dipping sauce (page 36) separately.

DAU PHU XAO XA
Stir-fried bean curd with lemongrass and chillies

SERVES 4

675 g/1½ lb firm beancurd (tofu)
peanut oil for frying
12 dried shiitake mushrooms,
    soaked in boiling water for 30
    minutes, stems trimmed, and
    drained, reserving 175 ml/
    6 fl oz of the soaking liquid
4 tablespoons hoisin sauce
2 tablespoons soy sauce
1 tablespoon tomato purée, plus
    1 teaspoon
2 fresh red chillies, finely
    chopped
2 leeks, white part only, thinly
    sliced and well rinsed
2 thick stalks of fresh
    lemongrass, peeled and finely
    chopped
1 red pepper, seeded and cut
    into 2.5 cm/1 inch squares
1 green pepper, seeded and cut
    into 2.5 cm/1 inch squares
pepper

Cut the beancurd into 2.5 cm/1 inch cubes and drain between double layers of paper towels.

Heat 2.5 cm/1 inch of oil in a large frying pan over moderately high heat. Carefully add the beancurd and fry, without crowding, until crisp and browned on all sides, about 8 minutes. Remove the beancurd with a slotted spoon and drain on paper towels.

Put the reserved mushroom soaking liquid, hoisin sauce, soy sauce, tomato purée and chillies in a bowl and stir to mix well.

Pour off all but 2 tablespoons of the oil from the frying pan. Add the leeks and lemongrass and stir-fry over moderately high heat until tender, about 1 minute. Add the peppers and mushroom caps, and stir-fry for a further 1 minute.

Stir in the sauce and the fried beancurd, then bring to the boil. Cook until the sauce thickens slightly, about 2 minutes, stirring frequently. Transfer to a serving dish, sprinkle with freshly ground black pepper and serve immediately.

Substantial enough as a main course, this vegetarian stir-fry also makes a great side dish. Serve plenty of steamed rice. If you like, start with a light vegetable broth.

CARI BO
Beef curry

SERVES 6–8

900 g/2 lb stewing beef, cut into
    5 cm/2 inch cubes
2 tablespoons grated fresh
    ginger
1 large onion, finely chopped
6 large garlic cloves, finely
    chopped
3 fresh red chillies, finely
    chopped
3 tablespoons curry powder,
    preferably Madras
2 teaspoons turmeric
1 teaspoon sugar
½ teaspoon ground black pepper
2 teaspoons salt
3 tablespoons peanut or
    vegetable oil
4 tablespoons fish sauce
4 carrots, cut into 2.5 cm/1 inch
    chunks
2 tablespoons cornflour
500 ml/16 fl oz canned
    unsweetened coconut milk,
    well stirred

Combine the beef, ginger, onion, garlic, chillies, curry powder, turmeric, sugar, pepper and 1 teaspoon of the salt. Cover and leave to marinate for 2 hours, or overnight in the refrigerator.

Heat the oil in a large, heavy-bottomed saucepan over high heat. Add the marinated beef and stir quickly to seal, about 3 minutes. Add 750 ml/1¼ pints hot water, the fish sauce, and the remaining 1 teaspoon salt. Bring to the boil, reduce the heat, cover and simmer until the beef is almost tender, about 1 hour.

Add the carrots and simmer, stirring occasionally, for a further 15 minutes.

Dissolve the cornflour in the coconut milk and stir the mixture into the stew. Continue simmering, uncovered, stirring to prevent sticking, until the sauce thickens slightly, about 15 minutes. Ladle the curry into a soup tureen and serve immediately.

Serve as a buffet-style dish, accompanied by steamed rice, rice noodles or French bread. A mixed green salad, tomato salad, or steamed vegetables would also be appropriate.

SUONG NUONG
Charcoal-grilled pork chops

SERVES 4

3 tablespoons fish sauce

2 tablespoons sugar

2 tablespoons peanut or
vegetable oil

2 thick stalks of fresh
lemongrass, peeled and thinly
sliced, or 2 tablespoons
grated fresh ginger

4 shallots, finely chopped

4 large garlic cloves, finely
chopped

2 fresh red chillies, finely
chopped

½ teaspoon ground black pepper

4 pork chops, about 2 cm/¾ inch
thick

Place all the ingredients except the pork chops in a
liquidizer or food processor and blend until finely
puréed. Transfer to a shallow dish large enough to
accommodate the chops in a single layer.

Add the chops and turn to coat evenly with the paste.
Cover and leave to marinate at room temperature for at
least 2 hours, or overnight in the refrigerator.

Prepare the barbecue or preheat the grill.

Grill the chops until they are browned on both
sides and just cooked through (the juices near the
bone should run clear when pierced with the tip
of a sharp knife), about 6–7 minutes on each side.
Serve immediately.

*Accompany these succulent chops with sliced fresh cucumbers
or Pickled vegetables (page 37) and steamed rice. Pass Chilli
dipping sauce (page 36) separately.*

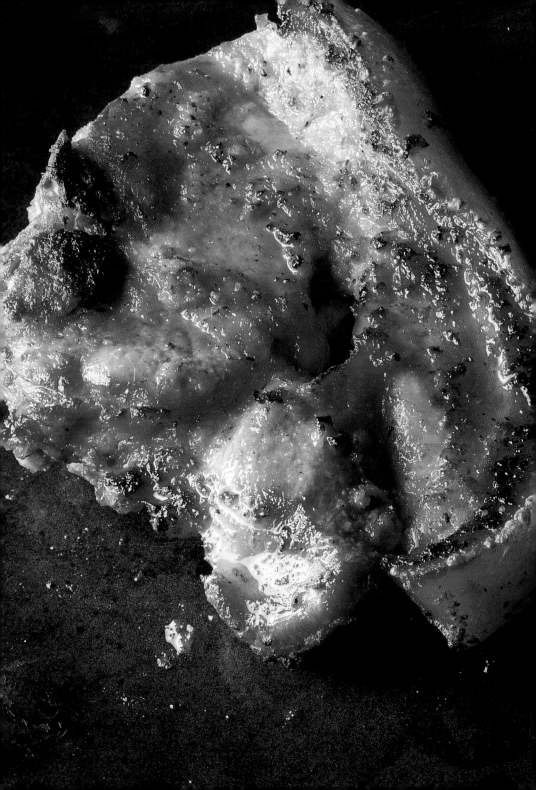

BO XAO KHOI TAY
Stir-fried beef with potatoes

SERVES 4–6

675 g/1½ lb beef flank steak or
    sirloin, cut against the grain
    into 3mm/⅛ inch slices,
    about 5 x 2.5cm/2 x 1 inch
2 tablespoons fish sauce
8 large garlic cloves, finely
    chopped
pepper
4 potatoes
1 teaspoon salt
peanut or vegetable oil for
    deep-frying
1 large onion, thinly sliced
1 tablespoon cornflour dissolved
    in 3 tablespoons water

Combine the beef with the fish sauce, half of the garlic, and some freshly ground black pepper and leave to marinate for 30 minutes.

Slice the potatoes about 1 cm/½ inch thick, then sprinkle the salt over them. Heat 8 cm/3 inches of oil in a deep-fryer or heavy-bottomed saucepan until very hot (about 190°C/375°F – a cube of bread should brown in 30 seconds) and deep-fry the potatoes until golden brown and tender. Remove with a slotted spoon and drain on paper towels.

Heat 2 tablespoons of oil in a large frying pan over high heat and brown the remaining garlic. Add the onion and the beef mixture and stir-fry until the beef is medium-rare, about 1 minute. Add the potatoes and cornflour mixture and stir briefly until the juices thicken. Transfer to a serving dish, sprinkle with freshly ground black pepper and serve immediately.

Accompany with rice or bread and a simple green vegetable, such as broccoli. A mixed green salad would be fine too. Pass Chilli dipping sauce (page 36) separately.

The Basics

GLOSSARY OF VIETNAMESE INGREDIENTS

These ingredients are sold in most Chinese, Vietnamese and Thai food shops, and are increasingly available from supermarkets.

FISH SAUCE
(*NUOC MAM*)

As fundamental to Vietnamese cooking as soy sauce is to Chinese and Japanese cuisines, this pungent liquid condiment, translucent brown in colour, is made from salted, fermented anchovies. It produces a magical effect on food, infusing whatever it is added to with a subtle, rich and elusive flavour.

PRAWN CRACKERS
(*BANH PHONG TOM*)

Also known as shrimp chips or *kroepoek* (in Indonesian), these feather-light wafers are delicious for snacks and as accompaniments to Vietnamese-style salads. When you buy them, they are translucent, reddish-pink or white, hard, thin discs; they must be fried in hot oil before serving. As soon as they are added to the hot oil, they will almost immediately puff up to triple their size.

dried prawn crackers
vegetable oil for frying

Heat 5 cm/2 inches of oil in a large frying pan over moderate heat. When the oil is quite hot, but not smoking, add the crackers, a few at a time, and cook until they puff up. Immediately turn them over and keep them immersed in the oil, using a slotted spoon, for 10–15 seconds longer. Do not let them colour, or they will taste bitter. Remove and drain on paper towels while you cook the rest.

Serve them the same day they are cooked, or store them in an airtight container for up to 4 days.

FRESH LEMONGRASS
(XA)

One of the most popular herbs in Vietnamese cuisine –
and one that gives Vietnamese food its unique character.
The grey-green, spear-like plant resembles an elongated
spring onion stalk with long, fibrous leaves. The lower
part of the stem has a white, slightly bulbous, meaty
base. It gives a marvellous lemony flavour to soups,
stews and stir-fries.

To use, discard any dried, tough outer leaves from the
stalk; trim the root end; slice paper-thin from the bulb
portion up to where the leaves begin to branch, then
finely chop to release more flavour during cooking.

DRIED RICE PAPERS
(BANH TRANG)

These very thin, dried pancakes, about 22 cm/9 inches
in diameter, are essential in preparing the famous
Vietnamese spring rolls. There is no substitute; thick
Chinese spring roll wrappers will not do.

Since they are very delicate and brittle they must be
handled with care. They tend to dry out and crack in
contact with air, so it is important to keep them covered
with a barely damp towel while you are working. To
use, they must be dipped briefly in hot water, then they
will become pliable within seconds.

GLUTINOUS OR SWEET RICE
(GAO NEP)

Also known as sticky rice, this differs from regular,
translucent, long-grain rice in that it has creamy white,
sturdy kernels. It also has a higher starch content, so it
needs to be washed, soaked overnight, then steamed.
Cooked, it forms a sticky mass, and has a slightly sweet
aftertaste. In Vietnam, sticky rice is a common breakfast
item, and is popular during holidays.

ROASTED AND TOASTED NUTS AND SEEDS

To preserve their fragrance, grind nuts and seeds only moments before using.

For roasted peanuts: place dry-roasted unsalted peanuts in a dry frying pan over moderate heat and cook, shaking the pan frequently, until golden brown and fragrant, about 3 minutes. Leave to cool. Grind coarsely in a spice grinder or food processor.

For toasted sesame seeds: place raw, hulled white sesame seeds in a dry frying pan over moderate heat and cook, stirring constantly with a wooden spoon, until golden brown and fragrant, 2–3 minutes. Leave to cool. Grind coarsely in a spice grinder or food processor.

NUOC CHAM (*Chilli dipping sauce*)

MAKES 250 ML/8 FL OZ

1 fresh red chilli, finely chopped
2 tablespoons sugar
2 tablespoons fresh lime juice
4 tablespoons rice vinegar or
　 distilled white vinegar
4 tablespoons fish sauce
2 large garlic cloves, finely
　 chopped

In a bowl, mix all of the ingredients with 4 tablespoons hot water. Stir to dissolve the sugar. Transfer to a jar, cover and store in the refrigerator for up to 1 week.

As this dipping sauce is omnipresent at the Vietnamese table and keeps well in the refrigerator, you may want to double or triple the recipe.

DUA CHUA (*Pickled vegetables*)

**MAKES ABOUT 1.5 LITRES/
2½ PINTS**

250 ml/8 fl oz distilled white
   vinegar
4 tablespoons sugar
2½ tablespoons salt
2 carrots, sliced 3 mm/
   ⅛ inch thick
675 g/1½ lb white cabbage
   or Chinese leaves, cored
   and cut into long shreds
   about 1 cm/½ inch wide
1 bunch of spring onions,
   trimmed and cut into
   5 cm/2 inch lengths

Put the vinegar, sugar, salt and 600 ml/1 pint water in a
large saucepan and bring to the boil, stirring to dissolve
the sugar. Remove from the heat and leave to cool until
just warm to the touch.

Put the carrots, cabbage and spring onions in a large
ceramic bowl and pour the brine over the vegetables.
(Cover with a small dish to keep the vegetables from
floating.) Cover and leave to stand at room temperature
until the vegetables turn sour, 4–6 hours or overnight.

The pickled vegetables will keep in the refrigerator for
up to 1 month. Drain before serving.

*These pickles are especially good with stews and grilled or fried
foods. Broccoli, cauliflower florets or green beans (halved
lengthwise) can be used instead of cabbage in this recipe.*

Classic Cooking

STARTERS
Jean Christophe Novelli Chef/patron of Maison Novelli, which opened in London to great acclaim in 1996. He previously worked at the Four Seasons restaurant, London.

VEGETABLE SOUPS
Elisabeth Luard Cookery writer for the *Sunday Telegraph Magazine* and author of *European Peasant Food* and *European Festival Food*, which won a Glenfiddich Award.

GOURMET SALADS
Sonia Stevenson The first woman chef in the UK to be awarded a Michelin star, at the Horn of Plenty in Devon. Author of *The Magic of Saucery* and *Fresh Ways with Fish*.

FISH AND SHELLFISH
Gordon Ramsay Chef/proprietor of one of London's most popular restaurants, Aubergine, recently awarded its second Michelin star. He is the author of *A Passion for Flavour*.

CHICKEN, DUCK AND GAME
Nick Nairn Chef/patron of Braeval restaurant near Aberfoyle in Scotland, whose BBC-TV series *Wild Harvest* was last summer's most successful cookery series, accompanied by a book.

LIVERS, SWEETBREADS AND KIDNEYS
Simon Hopkinson Former chef/patron at London's Bibendum restaurant, columnist and author of *Roast Chicken and Other Stories* and the forthcoming *The Prawn Cocktail Years*.

VEGETARIAN
Rosamond Richardson Author of several vegetarian titles, including *The Great Green Gourmet* and *Food from Green Places*. She has also appeared on television.

PASTA
Joy Davies One of the creators of *BBC Good Food Magazine*, she has been food editor of *She, Woman* and *Options* and written for the *Guardian, Daily Telegraph* and *Harpers & Queen*.

CHEESE DISHES
Rose Elliot The UK's most successful vegetarian cookery writer and author of many books, including *Not Just a Load of Old Lentils* and *The Classic Vegetarian Cookbook*.

POTATO DISHES
Patrick McDonald Author of the forthcoming *Simply Good Food* and Harvey Nichols' food consultant.

BISTRO COOKING
Anne Willan Founder and director of La Varenne Cookery School in Burgundy and West Virginia. Author of many books and a specialist in French cuisine.

ITALIAN COOKING
Anna Del Conte is the author of *The Classic Food of Northern Italy* (chosen as the 1996 Guild of Food Writers Book of the Year) and *The Gastronomy of Italy*. She has appeared on BBC-TV's *Masterchef*.

VIETNAMESE COOKING

Nicole Routhier One of the United States' most popular cookery writers, her books include *Cooking Under Wraps*, *Nicole Routhier's Fruit Cookbook* and the award-winning *The Foods of Vietnam*.

MALAYSIAN COOKING

Jill Dupleix One of Australia's best known cookery writers, with columns in the *Sydney Morning Herald* and *Elle*. Author of *New Food*, *Allegro al dente* and the Master Chefs *Pacific*.

PEKING CUISINE

Helen Chen Learned to cook traditional Peking dishes from her mother, Joyce Chen, the grande dame of Chinese cooking in the United States. The author of *Chinese Home Cooking*.

STIR FRIES

Kay Fairfax Author of several books, including *100 Great Stir-fries*, *Homemade* and *The Australian Christmas Book*.

NOODLES

Terry Durack Australia's most widely read restaurant critic and co-editor of the *Sydney Morning Herald Good Food Guide*. He is the author of *YUM!*, a book of stories and recipes.

NORTH INDIAN CURRIES

Pat Chapman Started the Curry Club in 1982. Appears regularly on television and radio and is the author of eighteen books, the latest being *The Thai Restaurant Cookbook*.

BARBECUES AND GRILLS

Brian Turner Chef/patron of Turner's in Knightsbridge and one of Britain's most popular food broadcasters; he appears frequently on *Ready Steady Cook*, *Food and Drink* and many other television programmes.

SUMMER AND WINTER CASSEROLES

Anton Edelmann Maître Chef des Cuisines at the Savoy Hotel, London, and author of six books. He appears regularly on BBC-TV's *Masterchef*.

TRADITIONAL PUDDINGS

Tessa Bramley Chef/patron of the acclaimed Old Vicarage restaurant in Ridgeway, Derbyshire. Author of *The Instinctive Cook*, and a regular presenter on a new Channel 4 daytime series *Here's One I Made Earlier*.

DECORATED CAKES

Jane Asher Author of several cookery books and a novel. She has also appeared in her own television series, *Jane Asher's Christmas* (1995).

FAVOURITE CAKES

Mary Berry One of Britain's leading cookery writers, her numerous books include *Mary Berry's Ultimate Cake Book*. She has made many television and radio appearances and is a regular contributor to cookery magazines.

Photographs © Simon Wheeler 1997

First published in 1997 by
George Weidenfeld & Nicolson
The Orion Publishing Group
Orion House
5 Upper St Martin's Lane
London WC2H 9EA

British Library Cataloguing-in-Publication data
A catalogue record for this book is available from
the British Library

ISBN 0 297 82287 X

Designed by Lucy Holmes
Edited by Maggie Ramsay
Food styling by Joy Davies
Typeset by Tiger Typeset